The Faithful Men Of God

Six Monologues Of Biblical Heroes

Lynda Pujadó

CSS Publishing Company, Inc., Lima, Ohio

THE FAITHFUL MEN OF GOD

ISBN: 0-7880-0763-7   PRINTED IN U.S.A.

To faithful men of God everywhere who know that God is their only strength, the One and only Commanding Officer, ruler of the universe and eternal, always patient and forgiving friend.

Table of Contents

Worship Service   7

Monologues   11

    Noah   11

    Abraham   15

    Joseph   20

    Moses   26

    Wise Man   31

    Chuza (Luke 8:3, 24:10) 35

The Faithful Men Of God:
Monologues Of Biblical Heroes

Worship Service

Call To Worship

P: Oh Lord, you are our mighty King!

C: **You come to us individually with your power and eternal
goodness. You raise us up with your strength to do great
things in your name. You challenge us to live faithfully to
you.**

P: You are our stronghold.

C: **We may come to you for refuge always. When we are desperate you are with us. When we are lonely, you console
us. When we are afraid, you have courage for us. You are
our friend. You are always available no matter who we
are, or what we are.**

P: You are ageless. You have always known us. You have always
been God.

C: **You are Elohim. Adonai. Jehovah. Yahweh. God. El
Shaddai. Lord. Immanuel. Wonderful Counselor. Mighty
God. Eternal Father. Prince of Peace. Lamb of God. Jesus
Christ.**

P: You created the universe. You created man in your image. You
gave us a mind, a spirit and a soul.

C: We seek to be close to you and to glorify you with everything that you have given us. We seek to glorify you with faith. We seek to glorify you in suffering. We long for your presence. We seek your peace.

P: God, you are always faithful to us! You love us!

C: We are weak, and we need you. We bow down to you. We belong to you and claim you as our own Creator God, Father and Eternal King.

Psalm 90:1-5 (This Psalm is attributed to Moses)

Second Lesson — Romans 5:1-5

Prayer Of The Church

Heavenly Father:

You have proven yourself faithful to people for thousands of years. You have always taken care of those who seek you and who want to belong to you. We belong to you, Lord, and we need you more than we realize. You know our minds and our thoughts, and you are compassionate to our lack of faith.

You are always with us and want to help us, but you demand faith from us. Give us the desire to come close to you and to yield our will and our spirit to yours. Help us to understand that no one who was ever faithful to you had an easy life, but found meaning in suffering.

We need your companionship. Help us to know you personally, and indeed, to bow down to you, Lord. Our will needs to be conformed in your eternal image. Our purpose is to bring glory to you. Our lives are not our own, but yours. Help us to live for eternity.

In Jesus' name, Amen.

Monologues

Noah

Hymn   "O Worship The King"
                                       (verses 1 and 2)

Abraham

Hymn   "I Know That My Redeemer Lives"
                                       (verses 1 and 2)

Joseph

Hymn   "A Mighty Fortress Is Our God"
                                       (verses 1 and 2)

Moses

Hymn   "O God, Our Help In Ages Past"
                                       (verses 1 and 2)

Wise Man

Hymn   "Lead On, O King Eternal"
                                       (verses 1 and 2)

Chuza

Hymn   "Take My Life And Let It Be"
                                       (verses 1 and 2)

Benediction

Noah

I was considered strange at best and at times mentally ill, I suppose. I know I was always isolated from society, but there was no other choice. I had no friends where we lived, and not only that, but my close and immediate family began to doubt my actions. I am a man used to being very much alone in society, and being with God. I am Noah *(bows)*. I had little interaction with others by personal choice. It was a time of great moral degeneration and falling away from God in our society. I didn't want to associate with some of the things that were happening near me and especially the bizarre moral behavior. I didn't want my family to be touched by the changing attitudes and lifestyles of the people. I must explain to you that concepts of right and wrong behavior were changing rapidly. At one point of time, there was a strong, definite moral code and sinful behavior was clearly unacceptable. To do certain things was considered shameful and a disgrace. To me, it seemed that what was once abhorrent in society was becoming more and more generally acceptable, and considered normal by the populace.

For this reason, I stayed away from them. I knew a type of awful fear when I saw these people that is difficult to describe. I felt that what they did was wrong, but worse than that, contagious. As an adult, I might be able to be firm in my convictions about what I believed in, but my children could be easily swayed into degeneracy. There were no strong godly role models for them to emulate anywhere.

At this turbulent, troublesome time, I believed in God and wanted to have a family that believed in God. I wanted to have a family that believed in prayer and strong faith as a lifestyle. It was becoming ridiculous and almost impossible to have this concept in mind when the rest of our society was mocking us and deliberately trying to get us to change to their patterns of behavior. Perhaps, you can relate to this situation, I don't know. But I could not dare let myself associate with any of the people near me because of my family. God talked to me then. As I said, I believed in God, but he had never been personal. This time, he talked to me and told me to build a ship. I am not a carpenter and we do not live near any large body of water. But, when you hear God's voice it makes an impact inside your soul, almost as though you are branded with his command. I could not and would not disagree with God, although it certainly did not make sense to build a ship and I didn't know how. God knew more about my capabilities than I did myself. He was extremely specific about the details of the ship and why I should build it. Everything that God said to me seemed unbelievable from a rational point of view, but I knew that God meant for me to be faithful to him at all costs.

I started building the ark. I built according to the private instructions that God had given me. People noticed, of course, what I was doing and taunted me. I continued and my building increased, the more they bothered me and humiliated me. Naturally, from time to time, I mentioned the God of the universe to these people. I encouraged them to consider their maker and redeemer and to yield their lives to him before it was too late. But, generally, they refused to listen and they laughed at me. The reason that God instructed me to build the ship was that he was going to destroy the earth with a flood and my family and I were going to be saved. He told me this, and I believed him and I proved it by my building, but it did not seem possible at all. I tried to explain the coming flood to my wife and sons, but they were skeptical. I knew then, as I saw them slowly slip away from me and the beliefs that I had in the God who was becoming more and more personal, that I was in trouble. I felt extremely alone and emotionally destitute. I had assumed that my family would back me up in the process of building the ship. I assumed they would understand the coming flood, but they did not. As I said in the beginning, they began to consider that I was mentally ill. They began to mistrust my judgments and tried at times to dissuade me from my project. If my children had no respect for me and didn't believe me, I knew they would soon join the rest of the society that we lived in which accepted deadly sin. I hurried.

Hymn

When the building of the ark was completed, I was instructed to bring in male and female species of all animals on the earth. It was my job to collect them so that they would not be removed from existence. It was not the animals' fault that the world was sinful. I also had to gather food for my family and the creatures so we would survive the ordeal of the coming journey. When I did this, I was in great personal peril. I was obeying God, but appeared mentally unbalanced to everyone else, and again, when I realized what was happening and all the opposition there was to my actions, I hurried greatly. People talked to my family about me. People discussed what they should do about me. Unfortunately, my wife questioned the validity of our relationship. She couldn't understand the profound course of faith that I was following. I momentarily considered that God had forgotten me and I was alone, with nothing or anyone to defend or support me.

I asked my wife and family to enter the ark. God told me it was the time. It was difficult for them, but they acquiesced, as though they were tolerating my mental deficiency. They disagreed with me about the plan to stay in the ark, and about the coming flood. I was surrounded by family members who were secretive and painful enemies. There was still nothing to indicate a worldwide, destructive flood, of course. It was just a normal day for us when we entered our new home. After everyone and the creatures were in, I locked the latch at the top of the ship and we were secure.

I don't really remember when the rain began, but it progressed with a fierce intensity. In the background, we could hear the desperate wails and crying of people we saw everyday. My family was adamant that we leave the ship and find shelter elsewhere. I said no. People flocked to us and peered inside our large boat. They wanted to come inside. They banged on the sides with their fists. We all looked at them. We saw their faces. My sons and their wives and my dearly beloved wife all stopped their discontented conversations. In shock, we witnessed the drama of suddenly desperate people who had mocked me for so long. By this time, the storm was in full force. I could not see much outside except for the variety of faces which were forced into our consciousness.

It was hard for us to grasp and comprehend the tremendous power of God. All we knew was that we were being spared. And, finally, nothing remained but the rolling ocean, the continuous raining universe and our ship. During the months of captivity on the ocean, we grew closer to God as a family. We prayed once again about our concerns and our fragile future. After many months, the rain subsided and our ship stopped moving on the ocean. We were brought to land. God gave us a rainbow as a beautiful sign to prove he would not destroy the earth by flood again. I felt a great peace inside me, knowing I'd have a new beginning with my family in a new earth. I felt we were spiritually renewed. I felt a deep, sacred longing for God's companionship.

I am Noah. I am not a carpenter nor am I a shipbuilder. I am a family man who believed in God and tried to obey him. God saved us and proved he was faithful. I do not know what will happen in the lives of my sons and their wives, or if they will be faithful to God as I would like them to be. That is not in my hands. We all have a new life now and a new beginning. My advice for everyone is to build your own ship and hold your family closely in it, away from the ravaging lifestyles of the world. Take command as captain, as God is your captain, and denounce evil. Sail on the sea of life always seeking God's direction and approval.

Abraham

In spite of everything that has been said about me as a man of faith, I haven't exactly been a perfect man. I want you to know that right now. I have made many drastic mistakes in my life. I don't know why God chose me as a man of faith. That had little to do with me. It was basically God's choosing. I am Abraham *(bows)*. God talked to me on different occasions and told me profound things, including many promises I did not understand, but I always believed him and did my best to obey him. God did not talk to anyone that I knew. He had not talked to my father. I tried to be worthy of God's attention, and wanted to be worthy of God's respect when he spoke to me, but I couldn't. I could never be worthy of God. I didn't know what to do. All I could do was listen attentively to God and attempt to discern what his purpose was for me in my life. In the beginning, God instructed me to take all of our possessions and travel to a new land which he would show me. He then gave me many promises. He promised to make a great nation from me. He said he would bless me and make my name great. He said I would be a blessing. I heard God speak to me, as I said, and I believed him and obeyed him when I was supposed to, although I certainly did not fully understand his meanings, or how he would accomplish his promises.

I have always been wealthy. I was born that way, and generally I took it for granted. My parents had many possessions, extensive property and numerous cattle. I married a beautiful woman named Sarah whom I love deeply, or at least, that is what I thought. We gathered all our estate together, our possessions and cattle, and traveled to the land of Canaan from our secure home in Ur in the Chaldeans. It was the will of God for us, and He had instructed us to do this. I had to leave everything I had ever known and it was extremely difficult emotionally. I don't think people understand how attached they are to their relationships and surroundings, whether they even like them or not, until they have to leave them behind. I had to leave my parental home and my relatives and face the unknown. I did this out of faith, because God said to do it. It wasn't my choice.

When we crossed the border into Egypt, the Pharaoh became impressed with the beauty of my wife. And, that is exactly what I expected to happen. I always knew Sarah was beautiful. He was even more impressed with her because she said she wasn't married to me. She did this because I told her to do it. I told her to save my life and risk hers, instead. I was afraid that if we went into the land of Egypt the Pharaoh would want to kill me to get Sarah, so I asked her to lie about our marriage right away. I didn't have to do that. I just did it for convenience. I did it so if there were any problems in Egypt, I would save my life at the expense of hers. As a result of what Sarah told him, Pharaoh took her with him. He wanted her as his wife. He had no intention of killing me, it seemed. But, when he heard from Sarah that she was not my wife, he was interested in her. And, he presented me with valuable gifts in fair exchange for the gift I had given him. I did not know what to do. Inside, I was deeply sorry for what I had done. The grief and sorrow which I experienced was so great that I wanted to end my life. But, that would not help Sarah at all. I had to face my crime realistically and completely. Surprisingly, it was the God of the universe who had claimed me as a man of faith who told Pharaoh the truth about my deception. I did not have the courage to do it. My wife was re-stored to me. I had to beg for forgiveness from her. I had no right to have her back. I had to explain that I had always loved her, but I was so scared that I couldn't think straight. It was not easy for me to do. I knew I deserved nothing from her. She could easily have gone back to her family where we came from, but she did not. She forgave me for what I had done. After that, I became much more respectful toward her and tried to be a better husband. I know I will never get over the shame I experienced as a result of what I did. My accumulation of wealth did not help me with integrity and cour-age in the face of danger. It was God and God alone who helped me when I couldn't help myself. I could not buy the courage I needed and will need in the future of my life to face danger honestly and openly.

Hymn   "I Know That My Redeemer Lives"

(verses 1 and 2)

One small point of contention between Sarah and me had always been the fact that we did not have any children. We both wanted children and certainly I wanted an heir. God listened to me and promised me an heir born in my own home. He said my descendants would be as numerous as the stars in the universe. I told Sarah we would have an heir but she became despondent because of her age when the subject of children came up. Unfortunately, she decided that in order for us to have an heir, it would have to come from her maid, Hagar. Hagar was a slave I had purchased for my wife. Of course, I had no feelings for the slave one way or the other. I listened to Sarah and I disliked the idea. But, I considered that she might be right. At any rate, I did not want to stand up to Sarah. I had no idea where I would get an heir if it was not from her slave, and so I took the slave, and she became pregnant. The slave and Sarah then became jealous of each other. Finally, her child was born. She called him Ishmael. He would be part of my household and would be my heir.

After the birth of Ishmael, God spoke to me again and repeated his promises. He also said that I would have an heir by Sarah. I realized that I had made a tremendous error with Hagar. As God promised, Sarah bore a child whom we called Isaac. I cannot tell you our delight over the birth of our son. Then, Sarah demanded that Ishmael and Hagar leave. She was furious when she realized that Ishmael would be part of my inheritance and an heir to the estate. She couldn't stand that. I didn't mind, but Sarah became enraged at just the thought. I sent them away into the desert wilderness. Although God had promised to bless Ishmael, I never saw either of them again.

Isaac grew into a fine boy. He was surrounded by constant attention from Sarah, me and our servants. Then, God spoke to me. His statements to me were brief and definitive. He told me to

17

sacrifice my beloved son who was so important in my life and Sarah's. I can't tell you the horror that filled my heart when I heard these words from my God. I did not understand why I had to do this, but my God was my creator and I had to obey. I cannot tell you about Sarah and her reaction. It was indescribably painful. If I sacrificed my own son, I would have no reason to live myself and I immediately considered suicide. I took the boy and some servants to the mountain in Moriah. I chopped the wood for the fire myself. I put it on my son's back and he willingly carried it. After all, my son loved me. I took a knife and we went up to the mountain together. At the top of the mountain where we would have our sacrifice, I asked my son to lie down on the altar where our sacrificial lamb would be. He was my son who loved me, and he obeyed me as I obeyed God. He did not understand. I bound him there on the altar; and we were alone. I raised my strong arm with the knife's sharp point aimed straight at the son I loved, with the intent to destroy him in obedience to God. At that exact moment in time, an angel of the Lord stopped me from going through with the sacrifice.

God wanted to make certain that I loved him more than my son, and I had proved it to him. It had been a severe test of faith. From that point on, God said that his eternal promises to me would start. I untied the knots that held my son on the sacrificial altar and told him about my deep relationship with God. My son listened to me, and together we went back down the mountain and returned to our home.

Faith is difficult to live by. It is not always easy to understand. Rules and regulations would be so much easier to live with. There would be so much less dependence on God for us, his people, and our lives would be more in our own control then. It is easier for us to believe that we know what is best for us. It has been said that I was a man of faith. Perhaps, but I cannot forget that I am a man who has made many mistakes. I would rather say that we have a God who is faithful to us. He is just, in spite of our human inadequacies and failures. I would say that it is our God who is faithful and gives unlimited mercy and loving kindness to those who call him their own. I pray that includes you and your family. I pray that you are in the family of faith and are numbered among my descendants as stars in the universe who live out their lives shining faithfully for their God.

Joseph

I am better than you are, aren't I? I assumed I was superior to everyone when I was growing up. I had been taught to believe that because my father Jacob treated me this way. He loved me most of all. I am Joseph *(bows)*. I always experienced exceptional attention and kindness from Jacob while my brothers did not. I automatically supposed that they did not get the attention I got because they were not as good as I was. For example, once my father gave me a special coat and I wore it proudly because I knew I was so deserving. I also had distinctly profound dreams showing my brothers bowing down to me. I didn't really understand the meanings, but the dreams pleased me greatly and I decided to relate the dreams to my brothers. They did not share my pleasure then, either. I did not do the same chores that my brothers did. I assumed I wasn't actually made for work like they were.

One day, while my brothers were tending the animals, my father instructed me to go and find them. As I came closer to them, they encircled me, as though I were surrounded by fierce beasts. They were insanely mad at me, and as I looked at them, I saw men I had not seen before. Their eyes blazed with unbelievable hatred. They ripped my treasured coat off and threw me violently into a deep pit meant to capture animals. They said horrible, unkind things to me. The shock of the situation almost killed me. No one had ever been allowed to do anything unkind to me before. I could feel the deep, hot earth against my skin and my throat raged with thirst as I lay motionless in the dirt which was swallowing me up alive. I thought I would die from the intense heat and thirst or from a wild beast that might fall in while prowling nearby. While I was in the pit, I could hear their voices above me, arguing. I kept thinking they would rescue me and things would be fine, again. I kept thinking that this was all a mistake. I had always had so much importance. I wanted my nice coat with me. I wanted them to give it back to me. It was mine, and I deserved it. I was so much better than they were — always so very much better.

Strangely enough, I was cruelly sold to some transient traders going to Egypt. I had been certain that I was going to die there alone in the pit of dirt and darkness. I couldn't believe that this was happening to me, but it was, and I had to take the pain. I was not better than anyone any more. I detested going to Egypt. I had to learn and adapt to a new language and culture. My position had always been so elevated and now I was a slave. I had to deal with the overwhelming pain of homesickness which plagued me everyday like an all-consuming, invisible enemy which wouldn't leave me alone. I often longed for my father's love. I pretended that my brothers did not hate me. I imagined that I would somehow see my father soon, as though he might suddenly appear to help me. I pretended that I was not in Egypt, but home where I belonged with my family. I cried frequently, but I masked my emotions and put them into working at my job. My master put me in charge of his entire estate and I worked diligently for him. Unfortunately, my master's wife tried to tempt me and when I refused, she went to my master and accused me of molesting her. Without any consideration for me, my master, who had trusted and respected me so much, immediately put me in prison. It was totally unfair. I was again thrown into a deep pit that seemed horrible beyond description. I could think of nothing good about my situation in life and often I wondered if I wouldn't be better off dead than alive.

I was put in charge of all the prisoners and I interpreted their dreams which disturbed them. I explained that wisdom for dream interpretation comes from God. I said it would not be my intelligence or interpretation, but God's. I had to let them know that God is supreme in my life. I explained to the men the meanings that I thought God meant them to have. They were released and I was again left alone and totally without hope or reason for living. I knew that God does not want us to take our own lives, but at this point, the thought of suicide became inviting. I thought that if there was any reason for me to be alive, I had no idea what it was. I wondered again if God had any concern for me at all. After a long time in prison, I changed. My physical appearance became very different. I couldn't shave. I was extremely dirty all the time and my skin had an unhealthy pallor about it because of lack of fresh air and sunshine and poor food. I was not a healthy specimen of a human being because I lacked so much of life's necessities. I didn't care about anything at that point, either. From my point of view, I resembled an animal more than the Joseph I had been earlier in my life. I did not dream anymore. I had changed so much and had so little hope that I gave up even my fondest imaginings. To me, my father and my brothers had died and so had I. I was dead emotionally and almost physically.

Without warning, it was demanded that I come out of the dungeon and present myself to the king. It seemed that he had heard of my skill at interpreting dreams. My mind had long since ceased to function normally because often I didn't know the difference between night and day. I needed an extreme calmness of nerves which I did not possess. I clung to the hope that my God had strength for me which I did not have on my own. I could not even walk properly. The fresh air, sunshine, and contact with normal people surprised me as a luxury I will never forget. I will never take for granted a normal day of life again.

Hymn "A Mighty Fortress Is Our God"
(verses 1 and 2)

Dreams plagued Pharaoh. He could do nothing without knowing their meaning. Before I did anything else, I explained to him that God gives insight and intelligence and that it would be God's interpretation rather than mine. I wanted him to understand that God should be the one to get credit for this, and he understood. I told Pharaoh that Egypt would have seven years of plentiful grain harvest and seven lean years. I told him he would have to provide for the years of famine by storing grain during the years of plenty. Besides, there would be a general famine on the earth and people from other countries would be coming to buy grain. At hearing the meaning of his dreams, Pharaoh became greatly relieved, as though a heavy burden had been lifted from him. He acknowledged the greatness of God. Then, to my amazement, he elevated me to second in command over the entire country of Egypt. I felt as though I was standing with God very close to me. Pharaoh took his personal ring off his finger and gave it to me. He treated me as his son. In due time, I was given a wife and we had sons.

It was with the birth of my sons, however, that I truly changed. I did not remember the cruelty of my brothers as I started to love again, devoting my life to my sons. My life had taken on a totally different perspective and the pain of my past had been removed. I had come to Egypt when I was seventeen years old and I had spent thirteen years in slavery. Now, I was second in command and had strong sons to live for. I also had become strong in many ways. I felt more compassionate and sensitive to others because of all the torment I had personally gone through. I had become willing to listen to and understand the problems of others. And, there was no way that I considered myself better than anyone or ever would again. However, I never lost sight of my God and the God of my father Jacob and his father Isaac and his father Abraham. My God was my God; then and forever and he would be the God of my children.

Exactly according to the dream God gave Pharaoh, the country of Egypt received seven bountiful years of grain harvest. During this time, I had our men store as much grain as possible. I had to remember the firm warning of God's promise that our next seven years would be famine. And, that is what happened. For the next seven years, we had very poor harvest yields and so did the rest of the earth. With our tall, full storage bins, our people were in no danger of going without food. Soon, men from other countries came to me, Joseph in Egypt, to buy grain for their hungry people. I praised God for giving us his wisdom to store grain so we would be taken care of.

During the beginning of the famine, in the first two years, I received a group of ten men from the land of Canaan who came to me to buy grain. They spoke Hebrew and were exceptionally polite to me. They all bowed down to me while expressing their earnest desire to buy my Egyptian grain. Of course, I had an interpreter between us, but, as I saw their faces again, and I listened more intently to their voices, I realized that I knew the men. I had seen them long ago in my lifetime, and in my dreams, but I had given them up, as they had me. They were my brothers. They did not recognize me, and for a long time, I did not let them know my identity. I spoke to them through an interpreter, pretending not to know Hebrew. It was a thorough shock to my emotional system and I had to be extremely cautious with the situation. I had to get control of myself immediately. These men were the men who had wanted me dead. They had hated me so much they had wanted to murder me. Many years had passed since my youth. Because of them, I had gone through so much suffering and horror which had been conquered only with God's grace, and now they faced me again. I didn't know what to do about them or, more importantly, what God expected of me now. At one point in time, I could not control my deep feelings and I ran out to find a secure, isolated room in which to cry out in loud, desperate sobs.

I listened to their conversations without their knowledge and realized that they had been haunted with guilt all these years by what they had done to me the day I was thrown into the pit. After much questioning and positive proof, I believed that we could be friends again, but it wasn't easy for me to get to this point. I had to learn about forgiveness and try to understand why they had done what they had to me. It was almost impossible for me to forgive them. I wanted desperately to see my aged father, Jacob, whom I had loved and whom I had given up. I finally had to disclose myself to them and to explain to them that they would be welcome to come to Egypt with their families and live. I cannot explain the emotions of shock, disbelief, and then gratitude that they experienced. All I knew was that I had to forgive them. And, I had to help them now when they desperately needed it. I had to put aside the grief, suffering, and desperation that I had known during my life and find purpose in it and bring glory to God because of it. I had to bring God's mercy to my family. I had to learn that it is not my place to judge others, or to take my own revenge. I didn't say I didn't want to judge or take revenge, I said it wasn't for me to do. I had to give the entire situation over to God.

Eventually, my family moved to Egypt. We are a united family again. It was done with God's power, and with God's guiding hand.

I never said that it was easy. God makes difficult demands on those whom he loves, but he also takes care of his own, although we might not know it when he is doing it. God has been with me in the most impossible circumstances and has never left. God is sovereign and just, and he cares about you more than you can realize. He proved this to me. He can to you, also. Don't worry if you are in the deepest problems of life. Worry if you do not trust God to take care of you, to be with you and to give you the strength you do not possess for your situation. God has everything that you need in this life. Trust him for it.

Moses

I had never wanted importance or a prominent leadership position. It never occurred to me. As a young man, I had the upbringing that was the best that I could have had under the circumstances. I am Moses *(bows)*. I was born to parents who were slaves to Pharaoh. We were descendants from Abraham, Isaac, Jacob, and Joseph. Our people have suffered hundreds of years in Egypt under pharaohs who were unkind to the Hebrew people after Joseph died. To keep me from being murdered, my mother put me adrift in the Nile River to see if I could be saved from Pharaoh's soldiers who routinely killed Hebrew infants. I was rescued and raised by Pharaoh's daughter. I had an elite existence and was highly educated. I did not experience the misery that my fellow Hebrew people had. I did not really know my mother or what became of her. I was of course acquainted with both the Hebrew and Egyptian cultures and I was born Hebrew, but I was raised as an Egyptian. One day, I saw an Egyptian hurting a Hebrew and I took it upon myself to kill him. I was young and immature then, and considered it my right to do that. Pharaoh found out what I had done and wanted to kill me. I ran away from Egypt, from Pharaoh's wrath, and from the murder I had committed, and I ended up in a desert wilderness called the land of Midian near the Gulf of Aqaba in the Sinai Peninsula.

I married into a nomadic family and had sons. I began the hard life of a desert shepherd. It was quite different from Pharaoh's palace, but I had little choice. I was a different Moses now and of course far more alone than I had ever been before. I had nothing but mere day-to-day existence and I lived as best I could. I am a man who knows extreme, almost unbearable aloneness. I knew Pharaoh wouldn't find me where I was because it was such a harsh environment, and that was what I wanted. One day when I was watching my father-in-law's flock, I noticed a burning bush that did not extinguish itself. It was burning alone in the desert. As I looked at it closer to make sure I wasn't imagining something, God spoke to me. I knew it was God almost immediately although I had not heard his personal voice before. When God speaks to you, you know it. His voice was clear and distinct.

He told me about himself, about the problems of the people of Israel and his plan for my life. I did not want to hear what he explained to me about his plans. He wanted me to return to Pharaoh and lead the Israelites out of bondage and to the land of Canaan. I was to be the leader of the Israelite nation. This idea shocked me. I did not want to do this because I was only a ragged shepherd living in obscure poverty. On a daily basis, I often knew hunger, loneliness, and obscurity and faced constant death from the elements or wild beasts. I had never considered myself a leader to a nation, and the idea seemed impossible. I did not have the ability, and I was terrified of the power of Pharaoh. I thought I would die in his presence. God performed miracles then in my sight to prove his power was divine. I pleaded with God about my inadequacy of speech. I thought God would give up his plan for using me then. I am not a public speaker and was hardly equipped to deal with leading the Israelite nation. But, God did not give up on that issue of my inadequacy, and decided to use Aaron, my brother, as a person who could speak for me.

I was a man running away from my past mistakes and I thought I had been successful. I had no choice but to obey the God who knew me there alone in the wilderness. I knew he was the God who created me and who had seen me my entire life. I belonged to him. God said he had heard his people crying in Egypt. He said he was going to deliver them. God was specific, telling me what he knew about the Israelites and Pharaoh. He was a very personal God whom I had not known before. He was a God who cared passionately about his people. I asked my father-in-law for permission to leave the home he had provided me and return to Egypt. I gathered my wife and my sons and explained to them what God had commanded of me. It was extremely difficult for me to do that. My wife had married a desert shepherd, not a leader of a nation. And, of course,

I also had the small matter of explaining to her about the murder I committed in my past which had to be dealt with. She hadn't known anything about that. My sons knew only about living in the desert with the flocks. From then on, God was the most important person in my life. My wife and sons had to yield to him and what he wanted me to do. They became secondary. It was not their choice to go to Egypt and see me become a leader of the Israelites; they were not Hebrew people and they had not heard God speak to them.

It was a long and treacherous trip back to Egypt. I met Aaron and we began our mission to persuade Pharaoh to let our countrymen leave Egypt. Pharaoh was a hard person to deal with and he always refused our requests. He wanted to own the Israelite people as part of his personal property and to do what he wanted to with them. Economically, Pharaoh had gotten accustomed to the convenience of Hebrew slaves doing so much work for his country, and he was powerful because of them. He knew his power came from domineering cruelty and he could not exist without controlling our people. I knew God was divine and only wanted the best for us. I knew God had more power than Pharaoh, but the man was insidious. He was evil in his dealings and in his intent. He had no regard for human life, and when we confronted him, I felt a chilling fear go through me. He was a human being, but did not have respect for life. I did not understand this. I don't know what, if anything, he respected.

Hymn   "O God, Our Help In Ages Past"
                                                (verses 1 and 2)

God proved time and again his own power to me and also as a sovereign God to Pharaoh. God sent him ten severe plagues which came over the country of Egypt as warnings of his supreme power. We told him God would do this. Each time, we warned him about a coming plague. Pharaoh thought he was more important than God. Each time he became concerned about the depth of the problem that overcame his country, but each time when the plague subsided, so did his concern about God's power. To me, there seemed to be nothing that would reach the man's heart, if he indeed had one.

28

The last plague that God sent to Pharaoh was one of death. We were instructed by God to tell the Israelite people to put lamb's blood on the doorposts of our homes and God promised to go through the country of Egypt during the night and kill the firstborn of every living creature whose home was without it. It was a night for us to remember always. Later, we called it the Passover because God's angel passed over our homes and spared us death. In the early hours of the morning, there were cries of horror heard throughout Egypt of people who had lost their firstborn child. Even Pharaoh's home wasn't spared. He awoke to find his son dead. At this point in time, Pharaoh faced a personal crisis and broke down. During this early morning, our people grabbed their belongings and fled Egypt. In deep despair, and not being able to cope personally, Pharaoh let us go. We were all on our way to Canaan, away from Pharaoh, away from bondage and to a new life with our God's direction.

As a people, we did not have organization. We did not have enough provisions. We did not have our route planned adequately. The people complained mercilessly. It seemed at times that returning to slavery under Pharaoh was their choice. They did not have the concept of faith in God, and at times their bitterness was unbelievable. God always listened to us and responded. He did grand miracles on our behalf. He provided personally for our needs. He was merciful beyond belief. For our direction, he gave us a cloud to follow during the daytime, and at night fire. God never left us, no matter how much we sinned. When the people complained constantly, I thought I would go insane as their leader. I was painfully alone at times. Prayer with God was my only safety net for staying alive psychologically. God never let me down, but he answered me according to his ways and his time.

God is the same today. The God who talked to me, Moses, in the wilderness is the same one who can talk to you no matter where you are, or who you are, or what you might be running from. I was a man who was hiding from my past and yet God had great plans for me. He has great plans for you, too, no matter who you are or what you have done, but you must obey him and live strongly by faith in his instructions. The God who led the impoverished and constantly complaining Hebrews away from Pharaoh can lead you out of your bondage, by way of faith's wilderness, and to God's own promised land for you and your family, whatever that might be. God bless you in your journey.

Wise Man

I come from the East *(points)*. You are probably not familiar with me or with my situation, but I do believe in your God, the God of the universe, the God who controls the heavens and who even has access to the minds of individuals. I am a wise man and astronomer *(bows)*. I followed a new star and found my savior and king, Jesus Christ, born in Bethlehem. My fellow scientists and I had been watching the night sky the way we always do. The position of the constellations and the birth of new stars fascinated us. It was our life. We were more concerned about observing the night sky and its activity than we were about the daytime sky. You would find this strange, I suppose, but that is our life. It became perfectly clear to us that we observed a new star, or star cluster. We watched and charted its progress with amazement. It was brilliant in its quality of luster, and it was moving faster than normal. It seemed to have a definite, predetermined course. More importantly, it commanded something inside me to follow it. Even though we were astronomers, we also believed in astrology. We believed that the birth of this star represented the birth of a new king or God.

My associates and I deliberated what to do about the phenomenon which faced us. The celestial body was moving fast, but we did not know where it was going. We had to decide what to do. For my part, I decided to follow it, and then so did some other members of my profession. We had to say good-bye to our families and explain that we did not know where we were going, or exactly why. For me personally, it was something inside me that I had to do with my life. And of course, I wanted to find the new king that the star represented. Everyone said we were wrong, irrational actually, to do this act. We left our jobs, and our safe homes, and our country. We faced a journey into the unknown. There was much criticism about what we were doing and how foolish we were to do it. But, I couldn't explain how I felt to anyone. I had to follow the star before it was too late. I felt that the king that it represented must be extremely important. The intensity of the star's brilliance and seeming power nagged at my consciousness night and day, and wouldn't leave me alone. We packed provisions for ourselves and also gifts that we thought would be appropriate for a king. Of course, we packed frankincense because in our country the growing and processing of this perfume was a major industry. It was an acceptable gift to someone of royalty. Our country exports much frankincense. We took myrrh balls and quantities of gold also to present to the king.

The journey was dangerous and we were not trained to defend ourselves against hordes of thieves that might attack us. We never knew what to expect. We studied the star's position every night and then we charted our course according to its position. We headed toward the country of Judea. These people have different customs than we do. Their language is different. We had to be careful as we slowly labored through the country because we didn't know how we would be treated as foreigners. Finally, we knew that our star was definitely over Jerusalem. We were pleased about this because King Herod's palace was directly under the star. We were sure he would know about this important matter and we decided to visit him. He listened to us but surprised us by saying that he didn't know anything about a new king being born. He was interested in our conversation about how we followed the newly born star, or star cluster, to Jerusalem, but he made no attempt to go out and find the star that we had so diligently become intimately acquainted with. He did not have the deep desire to know it as something supernaturally directed, as we did, and which we had risked our lives for. I did not understand this.

He wanted to know more about the birth of the new king, and we told him we would report back to him when we found him. We promised him and felt honored to have a conversation with him. We gave him our word and then we slowly left the palace. We were confused because we didn't know what to do. We were so sure that we had been in the right place when we went to visit King Herod, and we began to wonder if the entire trip had been a mistake. I began to feel sick inside myself because I had risked so much, had left so much, and had been so determined to follow what I thought had such importance. I wondered what to do. I wanted to do the right thing, but I didn't know what it was. At night, we watched our universe again as always. We realized that the star or bright celestial body had positioned itself over a tiny village near Jerusalem called Bethlehem and we went there. I didn't actually want to go there. It was just an unimportant village, and we were puzzled because it was no place for royalty. I wondered if it was just another stop for us, and another mistake. We were quite concerned because King Herod had absolutely no information for us at all about the new king, and we were so puzzled. We went to Bethlehem regardless and inquired locally about a new king being born. It was foolish to do this. It was only a small village. There were just local people about and I felt embarrassed. Our traveling companion, the star, was directly over a common house with just a young couple in it with a child. There had been people who mentioned that with the birth of this child the heavens opened up and angels of God had come out to speak to the shepherds. People said that the child was to be the Messiah, the eternal King of kings.

Hymn   "Lead On, O King Eternal"
                                   (verses 1 and 2)

This is the king we had been waiting for. We met the parents and knelt down and worshiped Jesus. He is the King of all kings. He is King over the universe and everything between heaven and earth, between the visible and invisible realm in which we live. We knew when we saw him that our journey had ended. I felt overwhelmed with joy, humility, and wonder as Mary his mother explained that Jesus is God's son. He is divine. Right away I decided we had to return to King Herod and report the news about God's son. You can't imagine my excitement! I wanted to tell everyone the news! I couldn't understand why he didn't know about the child. I thought that Mary and Joseph should have gone to him right away. That night, in a definite and profound dream God told me that we should stay away from Herod. He was an evil man and we needed

33

to return home by a different route. God talked to me inside my brain. It was so distinct that I couldn't do anything but obey. We left for home immediately knowing that we had an enemy who wanted to kill us.

I took a great and tremendous knowledge about God with me. He is a God who cares about me individually, and proves it. He saw us following the star which he created for the birth of his son and for us to study and follow by faith. He knew how we felt about the trip into the unknown. He was with us all the time! I brought this information and love back to my family in the east. I brought Christ and the gift of faith to my family. Of course, I continue to study the stars and the course of the universe. I haven't changed that. It has always been my pleasure. Now, however, I know who it is who controls the stars and the planets. I have met him. I have met the man of eternity. By following the star that begged at my heart and my consciousness, I found the God of the universe and I brought him to my family. Find the star from God in the universe called Jesus Christ and follow him at all costs, listen to God's voice of peace amid all the frantic noises of today and obey it, and make sure your family does also.

Chuza

It was business as usual in the palace. Herod Antipas, who is tetrarch over Galilee, entrusts me with his financial affairs and I am his personal financial adviser. I am Chuza *(bows)*. I know about his royal treasury and I make exact, detailed accounts of when and how the money goes in and out. I love numbers, accounting, and the fine mental detail that accompanies the work. I wouldn't want any other type of job and I consider myself well suited for this position. Naturally, I try to be extremely accommodating to my employer who is not exactly an easygoing man to get along with. But, he does trust me and I see to it that I do a good job. He should have every reason to be proud of my accounting skills. It is, after all, not easy since his numerous accounts are cumbersome to deal with. There are so many expenses you wouldn't normally even consider, nor would any of the general populace understand all the ways Herod spends money. I know how much he spends on his glamorous and evil wife, Herodias. I know the individual cost of just one of his joyous banquets and nights of revelry. I know the cost of Herod's wine in one year. I know what he pays his wine steward. I know what he pays his court scribes. I know what Herod pays his executioner to kill someone, or just to scourge someone, which isn't, of course, quite as lucrative. I understand the various complicated expenses involved in his large scale building projects, like the building of a new capital on the shores of the Lake of Galilee, for instance. I know how much his bricklayers and his construction supervisors are paid. I keep an even pace at my work and I do it diligently, no matter how vast the number of expenses that I am held accountable for and need to be aware of. I love the job even with all the complications.

At first, I didn't take much interest in the strangely wild and powerfully religious man called John the Baptist. There was no reason to. I am a man of reason and intellect, and my job demands a high social profile. This man was outwardly crazed. I am a Jewish man and observe our rules and customs appropriately. There is no way that I can afford to have any association with a radical and dirty religious fanatic. But my beloved wife Joanna paid attention to this man and became attentive to his teaching. Soon, I couldn't deny that he had a strong, spiritually inspired message of honesty for the Jewish people about repentance.

My employer had John the Baptist arrested and put in prison. Of course, I don't have contact with prisoners or the general public who come and go in Herod's presence. I do my work with zeal and keep to myself. But, it was this man who was preparing the public for Jesus, our supposed Messiah. After I heard John the Baptist speak, I considered him a genuine and powerful man of God, despite his unruly, bold appearance and seemingly antisocial mannerisms. The man had blatantly defiant courage that shocked Herod and most people as well. No one spoke or questioned Herod the way this man did, and Herod decided to have him murdered to please his deceitful wife. Joanna and I were sickened when this happened. At that moment, something inside of me changed, as though my heart were trying to find the heart of God wherever he was. I had always been a fine, upstanding Jewish man who abided by our rules. No one could deny that. But, this time I was so very sad and filled with remorse over my employer's actions that I wanted to do something effective for God.

Joanna soon began following Jesus and truly believed he was our Messiah. She witnessed miracles and believed in his words and in his kingdom of eternity. We lived a good life and our needs were few compared to most people. Many people who loved Jesus were desperately poor, weak, or ill, and he supplied their needs. We were not poor and our social position was elevated. At first, I didn't want to listen to Joanna's comments about Jesus because it was easier not to. But, soon, there were quiet whispers between us in the privacy of our home. My wife became a devoted and close follower of this man and his disciples. She knew his mother Mary well and was friends with her and other women followers. I loved my wife and we cherished each other deeply, but the fact that she believed that Jesus was the son of God became a problem for us. My employer was a politician and Jesus was a political problem. After a while, I also began to believe in and truly love this gentle man as God's son. It was undeniable to me and I wanted to be like Joanna and follow him everywhere. I could not. I was Herod's financial steward. I had my job to attend to.

Hymn   "Take My Life And Let It Be"
                                                      (verses 1 and 2)

Consistently, after diligently reviewing the statistics of Herod's budget, I often found surplus monies that were not needed. It would have been extremely foolish for me, as steward to Herod Antipas, to mention any of these small, insignificant sums to him. He would have been insulted and I would have lost my job. He was interested in political prowess, extreme, grandiose wealth and not petty sums. Time after time, whenever convenient, I channeled these extra, unneeded monies carefully into Joanna's hands for the work and needs of the disciples.

Suddenly, after the celebration of Passover, Jesus was brought into Herod's court, badly beaten. My head was bowed, as usual, doing the accounts in my private study. Jesus had to stand trial with Herod. There were no witnesses and it didn't take long. Herod gave him a guilty verdict and sent him back to Pilate. My head continued to be bowed, silently, as though I had no knowledge or concern of what was going on. Silent tears fell from my eyes and they smudged the parchment and my numbers.

Halfway across Jerusalem, outside of Pilate's court, you could hear the incessant raging of Jewish Pharisees who ranted demands to Pilate to crucify Jesus. I heard the crowd roar with hideous pleasure as I realized Pilate had issued the death warrant. I continued to do my job as though I knew and felt nothing, but my hands trembled and shook. Again, I could not control the tears of emotion that came from the depth of my heart. Before I had met Jesus, I had not realized that a person could have such great emotion or love. Now he was being taken away in grotesque horror and I could not bear to consider it. I felt then as though God himself were deserting the universe he had created.

It was as though I could feel and hear the footsteps of Jesus as he went to Calvary, as though he were making a narrow, invisible path in my heart for me to follow him. I had followed him previously, by allowing Joanna to be a disciple and by giving financially, but that was convenient then. There was no risk involved before, not like this. Now, it seemed as though the man that I had claimed as my beloved Savior was asking me to go to my own Calvary, and I felt filled with terror. I had wanted Jesus as my Savior, but I had not wanted my own crucifixion, and that is what I faced as I sat in my small cubicle trying to do my job.

I am an accountant. I work with numbers. I am a man of calculations. I did not understand the calling that Jesus of Nazareth was making on my heart. In the evening, when Joanna came home, she was uncontrollably shocked with sadness over the death of Jesus. She stated that she was going to his tomb with the other women as soon as our Jewish rules would permit it. I said nothing but only nodded in agreement. My mind was preoccupied with my own state of affairs with Herod Antipas. He could easily send soldiers to our home if he became outraged with Joanna's public appearance at Golgotha or acquired knowledge of my own personal dedication to Jesus. I waited, consumed with fear and depression, through the next day. I tenderly embraced my wife as she left at dawn to go to the tomb, wondering if it would be our own death sentence.

(Optional ending, if used on Good Friday)

When Joanna returned her ecstasy was unbelievable. All-encompassing joy radiated from her face, and then she told me the shocking news. Jesus, our Savior, was alive! I could not believe this! My mind had always functioned on an extremely rational level and this did not seem at all possible. He had died, this was an alleged fact, but he had left his place of burial and had returned to life again. She saw him. The other women saw him also. If I hadn't known my wife so well and trusted her completely, I would not have believed her. The look of extreme peace and tranquility on her face was indescribable.

"Jesus is alive! Do you understand what that means?" she asked me. "He has defeated death! There is life after death with Jesus. His kingdom of eternity is real. Do you understand, Chuza?" she demanded.

At first her words did not impact my consciousness and then I thought about them again. Jesus is alive! Our Savior is alive! His kingdom is real and death is only a transition to a majestic realm of existence with our beloved Savior. I reeled in this knowledge of eternal security.

Before I left to go to the palace to do my accounts, I suddenly remembered the Lord's invitation to carry my own cross to my own place of Calvary, whatever that might be. And, I knew as I walked out on the streets to the palace that I was carrying my cross. I could face what had to be faced because I believed that Jesus was God's son, only this time I knew that eternity was real. I opened the door to the palace and faced my employer, the man who had condemned Jesus my Savior and who could easily condemn me. I said nothing but bowed politely and felt the cross weighing heavily and putting deep spiritual scars on my back. As I went to my office cubicle, I knew that I was opening the door to eternity. Whatever happens to me from now on and wherever I am, I know that the Lord is waiting for me and that he is my eternal friend. I wear my cross every day. It is a precious burden and a personal decision. It is an honor. I plan to carry it until the day Jesus, my Savior and friend, takes me home forever. *(He leaves.)*

www.ingramcontent.com/pod-product-compliance
Lightning Source LLC
Chambersburg PA
CBHW071759020426
42331CB00008B/2322